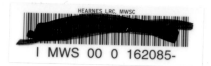
ALVIN TURNER AS FARMER

Alvin Turner
as Farmer

by
William Kloefkorn

Thanks are due to the following publications, in which many of these poems first appeared: *Aegis, Apple, Crazy Horse, Mississippi Review, Kansas Quarterly, Plaintiff, NEW: American & Canadian Poetry, Ark River Review, December, Prairie Schooner, Pebble, Road Apple Review, Midwest Quarterly, Poet and Critic, Omaha World-Herald, The Salt Creek Reader, The Small Pond, South and West* and *Wisconsin Review.*

This collection was originally published as *Road Apple Review*, Volume IV, Number 2, Summer 1972. It is reprinted with the permission of the editors of *Road Apple Review.*

ISBN 0–931534–02–X

for my granddad

"Only the man
who gives himself whole-hide to land can know
how absolute it is
to own. Or lose."

Bruce Cutler
A West Wind Rises

1 There is always the rock:
That, first and last, to remember.
The rock, at times at dusk the rabbit,
Robbing the garden in its own leaden way.
And I remember how once
I lost time deliberately,
Reining the team to a stop
And raising the rock high to crush it.
Underhoof it had wanted to trip
Even the full-rumped mares,
And I stood there in the furrow
With the rock raised above my head,
Powerless at last to reduce it
Or even to lose it to sight.
Yet I tried. (For in those days
I had not learned to say
There is always the rock.)
I threw it into the soft plowed ground
And dreamed that it disappeared.
How many times then it rose with the rain
I cannot say, nor can I boast
That ever its usefulness
Was fully cause for its being:
The fences failed to deplete it,
And it collared the hogs but partially.
Yet somehow I expected yesterday's blunted share
To be the last. That part which I cannot see,
I said, cannot reduce me.

2 It is afternoon, and hot.
I split the persimmon that last Spring
I felled and trimmed and sawed.
The wood is too green yet for the best burning,
And I am probably a fool
Not to wait for colder weather.
But I want the sight of something corded.
I'll arrange the stack on the back porch,
Using the house to keep it lined.
As an anchor against this southeastern Kansas wind
It should serve better even
Than the rock.

3

i'm sorry
i fussed so
much about those new
organdy curtains they
don't seem nearly so
expensive now
filled as they are
with this wild september
air you know
if i wouldn't have to push
our sheet away
and put something on and
if tomorrow wasn't
a school day
i'd wake the boys and
bring them in to see it
priceless!

4

So pshaw! the hogs went loose again,
And I can't blame a woman for saying
She is sick to the death of manure.
At a time like that even the mind
Goes muddied. (But she did very well,
That woman, hip-deep in muck,
Circling those hogs like a snake hunt
Closing in. And all the while
Going to the mud on her apron
To wipe the mud off her hands.
Manure, she calls it, and I don't argue.)
At such a time
The lifting of a single thread
Unhems the world.
The price of corn is up.
Hogs are down.
The next thing you know
The government will place a tax
On prayer. All this, and more,
As we change our socks
And put on new faces for supper.

5

Today the pace of the world is slow.
I can see it in the cows.
They come to their places at a single speed,
Stirring the morning sweetness of manure.
They arrive chewing to be yoked and fed,
To know again the touch of humanness
Upon milk-heavy teats. I lean my forehead
Against a warm tight-veined flank and feel
The quiet tremor of one cow's quiet mass.
Milk streams to froth between my legs,
Its whiteness thick with the effluvium
Of all grasses. Above her share
Of slubbered grain the cow chews on,
Wide-haunched; she is our grazing ground
Leisurely extending itself, until
Full-bellied and empty of milk
She with the others leaves
Her opened stanchion at a single speed,
Stirring the morning sweetness of manure—
And of flank and milk and grain and all pastures.

6   I need a wife.
So tonight I'll try some words
I practiced today in the hayfield.
        Because I want you
        on a leaseless,
        unbegged ground,
I'll say,
        where I can spread
        like ridges burst
        to hold you,
        I promise
        porousness:
        I will gather rain
        to store against
        your tendriled throat
        if
        on every side
        beside me
        you will drink
        and grow
        and clustering
        like the readiness
        of opened fields
        ripen yearly,
        daily yield.
        Martha Anderson,
I'll say,
        I love you.
        Will you be
        this farmer's wife?

7

I am ready now to admit
That I failed at everything
Except perhaps at one quick span
Of crisis, when I said yes
To my dying father and
To his only piece of acreage.
Gifts are not easy to accept,
Not when they nudge you to
The sudden wall of your stubbornness.
But at thirty I lay awake, alone,
Dreaming growth. I had failed
At everything, but when
I touched the land again
And heard my father's voice
I saw but one image:
Not the pondless pasture
Or the unpainted house
Or even the rock,
But a single seed.
I said, *Yes.*

8

The hill beside the house edits our world,
But it is good at least for runoff.
I'll have the new pond to the
South and west of the house,
Where I think it can catch
The most water. And I'll use
The dredged-out earth for dams.
I know that beneath this gumbo
The soil is red and reinforced with
Rock. It should hold the water
Very well and make a decent pond.
I'll start the work in the morning.
Today I'll do the final measuring,
Check the harness and
Sharpen the scoop.

9

The baby's cough was still in my ears
When I shot the rabbit.
Maybe that was why I found it so easy
To pull the trigger. We needed
Every peavine our plot could muster.
I don't know, maybe I
Should never have started farming.
I just don't care to see blood
On the lettuce. But the baby's cough
Was deep and going deeper,
And more than onion soup seemed necessary.
So I shot the rabbit again and again,
Sliding a deheaded stove bolt
Down the barrel to dislodge
The smoke-smeared casing. Then
In winter the blood was bright
Upon the snow as I anticipated
Spring. But the rabbit
Was always there, like the rock,
Singular as buckshot. Still,
I did what I could to save the garden,
Even long after the baby was buried.
We needed its savings for other ailments,
Other medicines. So into the seasons
I fought the rabbits,
The chamber of my .12-gauge
Like a little throat, coughing.

10 I live mostly now in photographs,
Glossed by the glass of quaint dry cabinets.
In one (most recent) I stand beside the house,
Loose inside my overalls.
At my left the house leans north,
Unpainted as the day I first restored it.
Beyond and to the south an edge of pond
Reflects the low sun's light.
A walnut tree looms nearly leafless,
And beneath me breeds a rock.

I posed for this one.
That is why I am holding my hat.
I am in the center of the picture,
So small that I have lost all easy faith
In human weights, in human measurements.

11

This morning I am dizzy
With the plump brown evidence of fall.
The granary is full.
The bucket at the cistern glints its use.
The baby is solid as a tractor lug.
In the kitchen
Martha glows fuller than her cookstove's fire.
I want a dozen pancakes,
Ma'am,
A ton of sausage,
Half a crate of eggs,
Some oatmeal and a loaf of toast.
Feed me,
Woman,
Then kindly step back!
I intend to do some pretty damn fancy whistling
While I slop the hogs.

12 Martha says that all the rivers
Run to the sea,
Yet the sea is not full.
I have trimmed a new wick,
And beside its even flame
Martha reads aloud,
Her voice clean as mopped linoleum.
Pshaw, I say, needling,
What has that to do with downspouts?

> (I know that she wants the baby baptized,
> And I don't really care, one way or the other.
> Our first child took her rebirth
> With her to the grave,
> So that I'd personally rather see
> The water on the corn, or not at all.
> But I'll not be muleheaded.)

She looks up briefly, not answering,
Then reads that there is no new thing
Under the sun. I nod,
Meaning that I shall arrange the baptism
For the earliest Sunday.

> (I wouldn't mention it
> In town at the feedstore,
> But Martha's voice by lamplight
> Is worth at least one waste of rain.)

13

I am a dirt farmer
Who dreams of poetry.
Is that so strange? Is anything?
I have bent myself thankfully
Over the heat of cowchips.
When the lespedeza flowers
I breathe its blooms.
The calf I winch to birth
Grows legs like oaks to graze on,
And stuck hogs bleed for breakfasts.
This morning at milking
I kissed the cow's warm flank
And she kicked the milk to froth beneath my knees.
I forgave her,
Then cried with the cats.
Now the manure is in bloom,
Thistles defend the driveway,
And corncobs gird the mud beneath my boots.
Plotting harvests,
I roam my acreage like a sweet spy.

14

New canvas for the combine:
It had to be done,
Though the boy's shoes turn to skin.
Can't a woman understand
A simple thing like that?
Each man has his own machine
To keep in tune, I say,
And I don't like to think
He has to sacrifice one vital cog.

But somewhere the message gets confused,
And I'm blamed if I can make it right.

So the children walk our shards on bloody feet
While father, fat on canvas, dissipates.
She seems to see us so, at any rate,
And when she sighs and gathers up her yarn
I try again.

I love the boys like they were fanbelts,
I say,
And brand new.

15 After a difference
We go together as
We fall apart: with words.
They are clear and clipped and
Gently strange,
And hearing them I think
Their sound is like the little noise
Of needles, knitting.

16

Under transient skies
I cannot hobble change,
Not now or ever.
My mares grew flywheels
One long summer night,
And yesterday my boys
Stood taller even than their trousers.
Yet nothing near is ever going to die,
So when Martha asked to see the doctor
I laughed, seeing that she tried to.
I called him to the farm,
Where from that day an order shifted.
Now Martha lies on the duafold,
Absorbed by its podded leather,
And I have made my pallet beside her.
At night the straining of the stove
Outpops her breathing. But
Something more than heat is on the air.
Long into the night I lie awake,
Hoping to see it in the slits of fire
Or smell it in a wisp of charred persimmon.
Beside, above me, Martha disappears.
Can that be it?
Not the knowledge of her cancer,
But the noise of falling flesh?
Long into the nights I lie awake,
Working my ears like a watchdog.

17

Perhaps one of Ecclesiastes' rivers
Does somehow begin at our downspouts,
And if I mended them as well as I meant to
The cistern should be bursting.
I have never seen such rain, the rocks so clean.
Because I prefer not to think of mire,
Of the chores of evening,
I'll settle back
And contemplate the woman.

I see her with a dishpan
Catching rain. She wants the water
Straight from heaven, untainted even
By my soldered tin. With it
She will wash her hair,
With it rub her clear face clearer.
She has a small nose,
Active eyes,
And a high forehead that
Under a wrap of hair shampooed
Will smell like rain.

Later I'll use a kiss. But
With words I reach to touch it now:
Lightly, like the skimming of cream.
My hand to her brow,
My fingers,
Tipped in butter,
Suddenly rich and unpalsied and newly nerved.

18

look boys
i don't honestly know
whether jesus wants either of you
for a sunbeam you'll
have to check with your
mother if you must have
my opinion though
i'd guess he has
plenty already like
for instance that one
there on the knifeblade
which by midnight
just might be
sharp enough to saw
lard if you two bandits
will keep the grindstone
wet
you hear me?

19

On a clear night
The larger rocks are reptiles.
One, a turtle, is creeping
From the east toward the house.
Robert saw it first, and named it.
It is not dangerous, he said,
Unless you spur it in the flank.

On a clear night,
Backgrounded by the grunting of the hogs,
He rides the rock,
Escaping Andrew.
I sit on the high east porch, watching.
Martha's hands, in the adjoining room,
Are clapping harmony.

On a clear night
I see so sharply that
The barbs upon our taut and endless fence
Amaze the eye. They guard like little girdles
This evening's flatulence.

On a clear night
Emptiness is maverick, out of mind.
Look, boys, I say,
Our moon is a Holstein rising from the pasture,
Her belly full as a tick.

20

So darkly cold
the birds dream feathers.

But in the lamplit kitchen
evening simmers.
Martha stands at the stove,
her body like a wide bed
blanketed in apron,
sampling broth.
The lips she jeopardizes
jump like nerves
to the touch of tablespoon.

Supper, she says, is ready.

So while outside
the birds dream feathers
inside the potato soup
is warm with faces.

21

I am trying now to think of how it is,
Of how a man reaches with both arms
To describe a world. I watched my father die,
Said yes to his request, and in that single word
Sent all my sinews, like a measurement,
Around this quarter section. All else has been
A hanging on, a hoped-on fallowing,
So that each time the fence goes slack
I tear good flesh to snug it.
I want to keep the cattle in,
My lean brimmed world unspilled. Neighbors,
    relatives,
D. S. Simpson at the feedstore—
All are at last outside.
With them, at times, I pick my teeth.
I need their help, their mash.
But when against a January wind
The screendoors flap their grainsacks
And lampwicks jump their light like nerves
Against the wallpaper, I sense the breadth
Of chattels. At times like these
The cattle cluster, hugging the hill.
The horses, in their leanto, stamp untethered.
A soughing in the windbreak sends the chickens
To an early roost. Within the fence
Each farm-part reaches out its arms
To hug itself, and what it puts
Its fingers to is what it cares for.
It seems to be a fact:
When the trough is low
Epiphanies show sharp as store-bought shares.
They are few and forever, it seems,
And trying now to think of how it is
I see the late fall rabbit
That disappears each hunt into
Some stark plum thicket in the pasture.
Thinking: it is not magic, after all!
Somewhere, even then, the rabbit trembles
In his camouflage.

I am now that rabbit.
Silent and cool and moist-nosed,
I crouch naked under all fur,
Augmenting in my merest mortal way
The mercy of the hunter.

22

Restless
In the pine soft night
I rise in search of woodpiles.
The air is well mooned,
Iced and clear,
The axblade silver sharp.
I select a stump, crosscut
And frozen dried.
Ungloved, I finger
Heft and balance.
Patiently.

Now at last it is time.

The upright wood stays stiff
Against the final moment
As my strike calls out
A quick curt simple sound.
The wood splits clean.
I bend low over it, the halves
Bloodless, fresh,
Aromatic as matured pipes,
And, between,
A birth of air
Filled with the white frost
Of my own raw breath.

I sleep now like a child
Clutching a new nickel.

23

At the sink Martha outhustles the dusk,
Bending herself to the washing of lampchimneys.
I have never seen a woman so quick, so deft.
Within a porcelained pan of suds
She turns the smoke-dark glass,
Lifting it at last
Into the dry bright rub of dishtowels.
And I am struck with the crisp, clean motion of it all,
With how it happens so concordantly:
At the stroke of dark
The fitting of one new chimney to each new flame,
And our settling into nightfall
Like globes of glass no thicker than a shim.

24

I stand alone at the foot
Of my father's grave,
Trembling to tell:
The door to the granary is open,
Sir,
And someone lost the bucket
To the well.

25 Our latest calf has found its legs.
Behind a slatted gate
the boys look on, laughing.
Today the world is upright,
blue-headed and fine and clear as quartz.
Don't all men, some time or other,
deserve such openings?
The milk has gone its rounds,
from cow to separator to calfbucket,
and the boys, who steadied it
against the calves' impatience,
have gone glandular with advantage.
They are both old men now, and wise.
They cannot remember ever wobbling.
They spread their breakfast sorghum by themselves.
Barefooted, their leaning into life
is like a breeze to cheekbones,
and watching them I feel my strength
go doubled, my shoulders rippled
with cords toughskinned to time.

                    O Lord,

How sweet to be free of the cradle!
To walk cocksure a furlong of bunch grass
as if it were boundless, and bottom land!

26 Though this house has newer than puncheon doors
There seems never an end to chinking.
Last night beneath a wealth of quilts
I heard a rat gnawing.
There was first a scratching at rusted tin,
Then the fine flaking of pine.
I thought of waking Martha,
Of chancing a snap of the shotgun,
But changed my mind.
The rasping steadied to a drone
Until sunup brought our silent boys to breakfast
From their shivering room.
It was exactly as I had feared:
Robert was missing one ear.
Half of Andrew's nose was gone.
In the north kitchen wall
A hole the size of a hayrick loomed.
And at the center of the table
A fat rat,
Slickskinned as oilcloth,
Peered out with little lizard eyes,
Its second helping sure as death and taxes.

27

So we placed him publicly
For moments
Inside a church
(Having contractually arranged for
The removal of his manured boots)
Then sat still on arid stony pews
To hear a file of words
Tell us to care, but
Not to care—while
Among lilies
My father's
Huge hands
Lay like a poultice
Upon the stomach of some
Slight discomfort:
　　　The burning of unfamiliar shoes, perhaps,
　　　Or the embarrassment at wreaths;
　　　Or the scent of the effluvium
　　　Of loved ones, being nursed by the drone
　　　Of a friendly family physician
Back to death.

28

Not even on the Sabbath
Can we leave the chores to heaven.
I mention this to Martha.
She tosses off a smile, not breaking stride.
It means we better hustle
Or be late for Sunday school.
Between breakfast and
The stripping of the cows
The house releases redolence.
The boys smell of yesterday's homemade haircuts,
Their talcum hovering like halos.
Martha clouds the air with stout sachet.
Into it all,
Like a bull sideboarded for market,
I stomp my barnyard boots,
Throw water to my hair and face,
Then towel it downward,
Dripping from the elbows.
The day, familiar as a necktie,
Turns like an auger in a woodknot,
And during the testimonials
I knead my chinflesh into dough,
Stanching sleep.

I sometimes fail.

Last Sunday in the center of the sermon
I tacked canvas to the hen house windows.
Three roosters, shivering, applauded,
And I looked up to see
Christ like a pea-eyed whirlwind
Sitting on a buckboard.
Are you Job? he asked.
No, I said, he lives one farm to the north.
You'll know him by the pockmarks on his face,
And by the holy stitching through his mouth.
I invited the voice to dinner,
But before I heard an answer
Its form had grown comb and feathers.

I awoke to the singing of a strange salvation
And to the shaking of weekly hands.

29

The cats too congregate
at milking time,
discovering their own
firm ritual in mine.

Together we make a church of it:
I and the cows and the cats,
and the flies that swarm like music
at the worshippers' backs.

> With careful hands
> I direct a stream of milk
> into the mouth of
> one soft beggar.
> In the midst of steaming dung
> I am more than priest:
> confessor to cats,
> I sit in total ignorance,
> intermediating only substance.
> Alpha and Omega are
> somewhere in the pasture, perhaps —
> perhaps playing brackets with lives.

I couldn't care less.

> I have my cats and my cows,
> my horde of bandied flies.
> Barnlife. Shinglesmell.
> The thick slobbering of grain.
> And the milk that squirts
> from one mystery to
> another, and back
> somehow
> some way
> some time
> again.

O brothers and sisters!
The meaning all is here—
here in the barn and the milk.

30

Outside the kitchen window,
On the unpainted seeded shelf
Of this year's feeder,
Lies a dead wren. I see it
Incidentally
Over an early winter breakfast.
A north wind spreads the feathers
And animates the grain,
Of which no single seed
Is larger than a bird's eye.

I hurry with egg on my chin into the bedroom.
Martha!
I cannot soon enough uncover you.
To watch you blink again.
To hear you fret. To part your hair.
To kiss the stretch marks on your stomach's skin.

31

Both boys alive and well.
Both fed, asleep.
And Martha strong again,
Straight as a rakehandle.

On this warm evening
We lie beside a rock,
Taming locusts.
I am corpulent
Inside new overalls,
And pressing my woman
Against the rock
I sense the depth of flesh
And all at once I know:
Only the rock
Describes such tenderness!
There is always the rock,
I say for the first time,
And tonight, Mrs. Turner,
There is also you.

32

The tiptoeing of final ledges
Should prepare us for routine ones.
Yet I have never not been angry
At the breakdown of a hinge.
It seems as though each door
Awaits the blinking of an eye:
Then pins like slim Houdinis
Slip their grooves,
And padlocked hasps run empty.

Yesterday we buried our daughter.
She was not much larger
Than a bar of soap.
We stayed until the end
To view the closing of the gravedoor.
And sure enough:
The long-shadowed afternoon,
And the bumpy road returning,
Gave the granary time:
Its door had dropped a hinge.
In the wind a sudden flapping
Shied the mare,
And seeing what had happened
I swore lightly,
My anger like a new nerve
Fumbling for a hammer.

Through the awkward gap
I could not see the predators,
But something silent told me they were there.

33

Sometimes dark clouds skirt the hilltop,
Turning like slow-motioned discs
In the direction of town, and
So low their trailings nearly touch
The housetop. From the southwest
A damp wind rises.
At such a time
We somehow seem to know
If more than rain portends:
Invisible ticks go burrowing
Beneath the skin.
Almost without words then
We huddle our green humilities,
Dropping life in mid-work
To abide brief burial
In a lamplit cave.
Martha superintends the light,
The extra kerosene.
I with an axe work the cavedoor's pulley
And muster the boys.
                              Thus
Amid undusted beets,
The patient jars
Of corn and peas and peaches,
We await the wind,
And I remember clearly how it was
That final time
We found ourselves together.
It was like the late-stage ripening
Of a tiny clan:
Robert and Andrew, grown quickly men,
Wearing their mother's massive hair,
Their beefy tight-fisted arms
About to burst
Beneath the rolled-up sleeves
Of cotton shirts.
I had to acknowledge
That this cave could not much longer
Keep us all,

And it was the boys themselves,
Itchy inside their workclothes,
Who chiefly said it.
I had known their restlessness before,
But in the cave that certain Spring
I fingered ripeness
That no meager rocky ground
Could quite contain.
We said nothing about it,
At the time.
The wind was at its highest, shrill as hogwhines.
Martha, in the midst of her cannings,
Sat silent. The boys in workboots
Toed the earthen floor.
And having told them both goodbye
I walked with mothlike strides
Into the lampflame,
Flickering.

34

Company.
One is a child, a girl.
Almost my own.
Do I know your daddy?
It seems I do.
His name is Robert Turner.
(Gently he slipped the traces,
Sweetheart,
Grazing his way to war.
Now like a peaceful general
He brings fresh curls
To inspect these feedshocked acres.)
I'm sorry the house is such a mess.
Yes, those are horse droppings
On the linoleum.
But make yourselves at home.
Robert, let's walk the acreage.
You come along too, young ladies.
I'll show you a new milkstool
I hammered together this morning.
Then maybe I'll saddle the pony.
We can all talk at the same time,
If you want.
You know how it is.
The days are short this time of year,
And growing shorter.

35

With rope/chain/wire/terrets
I jerrybuild a halter for the rock.
It is the largest in the yard,
A nuisance rising like a single blinder
Between the house and driveway.
With double lengths of cable then
I join the rigging to a singletree
And give the mare her neck.
Breaking her knees, wide Mollie
Snaps the slack and
Lurches fetlock-deep with strain,
And splitting an obedient morning with commands
I feel the earth begin begrudgingly to move.
There is then no stopping:
The boulder, like a blunt-shared plow,
Eats out a furrow deep enough for tourists.
Across the lane the muscle-rippled mare
Gutstrains her load, until
Beyond the narrow roadway's shoulder
I scissor back the reins
And shout a halt.
One second's echo: then
The new-homed rock groans into place.
The mare, high eared, breaks wind.
And Martha, on the south-porch steps,
Is on her toes,
Clapping like a congregation,
Her face appled in sunshine,
Her stomach firm as a melon
With our first child.

Over coffee I am more than horseflesh,
And profound.
What you cannot destroy,
I say,
You pissant
To a more convenient ground.

36

hush
little one
that racket
in the kitchen
is not a new war
or the rattling
of dry bones
joining
at the second
coming it is only
your infinite
mother
with her masher
humbling the
potatoes

37

Andrew.
Trailing Robert
He got so used to galloping
He dropped the checkreins.
So I am not surprised
That he has taken to teaching school.
As a boy
He used to chew his tongue
Late into the evening—
Reading, figuring,
Burning his shoes
Against the banking of a coalfire.
Which puts in mind an equation
I must try to remember
For his next visit.
If last year's leafing is compost,
Why now is the scorching of footwear
So tart, so sweet?

38

I remember thinking once
That if mother were a fencepost
Our cows would have an easy time of it,
Grazing the fence down.
Though I was the only child she had
To entertain such thoughts,
I meant no disrespect.
It was simply this:
Mother's frailty was a daily fact,
So that her dying was no more strange
Than my drawing of another breath.
It is no disgrace to be adzed away,
Beneath the grinding of restless teeth
To say, *Enough.*
When the parings outweigh the person
It is time to try something else.
So mother died,
And the farm did not miss a lick.
We buried her in town,
Among acquaintances,
Nailing a length of one-by-eight
Against a freshly-trimmed hedgepost
To mark the grave.

39

In the midst of shingling I see Jehovah
Tumble from the Pearly Gates
Into the chimney,
And because I have a certain
Compassion for the gods,
And a desire to keep my flue clean,
I resolve to haul him out.

With fingers as wings
I balance my way to the jut of brick.
Into the small twilighted hole,
Like a windowpeeker,
I stretch my neck,

And there unreasonably below
Is a young sparrow,
Testing its feathers
Against a sooted wall.

I return to my work,
Shingle until dark,
Then rescue myself with a ladder.

40 *Dust to dust*

is little consolation
as I look this evening
toward the fieldcorn.

I should be grateful, I suppose,
that it is feed, not flesh, that's browning.
Yet I swear the two have more in common
than the weatherman predicts.
Another dryland weekend:
and this will surely be the straw
to break a farmer's back.

The thought is more than weary metaphor.

That must be why
the hollows at my spine
are tender to the touch,
and why the fingers
lying in my lap
are curling.

41

At the height of this late day's sun
I spy a large rock,
And flexing myself
I dedicate its bulk
To whatever errors there are
Inside me.

I roll up my sleeves,
Approach the rock and with inclusive eyes
Size it slowly.
Three ton, I say,
Thinking conservatively,
Then eating air like vitamins
I inch the burden upward
Upon my back.

With each deliberate step
The dry earth cracks.

I toil the hill
Through every season,
Crowning one gradation
Only to confront another,
Until near sundown
I walk at last along the top.
Carefully then I ease the burden down.
It settles against the earth
As though it had never left,
And when it is heavily in place
I notice other rocks around it,
Where, under a slant of sundogged light,
Behold! The hill blooms monuments.

I go to my knees, then,
To kiss the ground.
At such a time
Our lips are grateful
With their love,
Their mutual guilt.

42

So much seems merely preparation.

I use the tools I have
To shape the tools I think I'll need
To do the work
That surely must be done.

Yesterday, with nuts/bolts/knuckles,
With plates of rusted steel,
I dehorned
Two young steers,
Stanching their blood with black salve
Thick as wheelgrease.
Today I scavenger the rods
I'll shape to neckyokes for the milkcows.
Tomorrow, I suppose,
The hill will show a hairline crack,
And I'll be back to pacing the acreage—
To combing its junk like a springtooth,
Looking for a reinforcement
Half a mile long,
One that can serve as both bit and bolt.
Slowly through the hill
I'll twist the threaded rod,
Then using lockwashers
Snug the nut
Until the crack relents.
If every accident goes well,
The hill should last
At least
Another
Year.

43

friends that
fresh-braised pork
you're licking chops
to was on the
hoof a week ago
rooting rubbish
with the same
nostrils i chose
to fire the rifle bullets
into that act being
only one of god's
manifold mysterious
ways for which
on this november day
we all should probably
give thanks
amen!

44

We have slapped the ponies out to pasture
And now, walking the fence,
Boys, I say, I dub you men:
From this hour forward
Do your coloring here.

Robert, dragging the hammer,
Chooses a deep blue for the grass.
Andrew, his pockets rife with staples,
Yellows every rock.
Suspending a hand above the pond
I fancy the water pink.
Our house goes green,
The improvements red as cockscombs.
Then with crayons sharp as augerpoints
We trace the fenceline black,
Until the farm is bordered
Like a page.

Well done, I say,

And back over the hill
In single file
We march,

To live in the little green house.

45

When the sap starts downward
Farmyards sigh,
Their sound the drone of deliverance that moves
Like half-slept moments
To the first shrill hour of Spring.

It is the relief of closing in,
The disconnection
Of leaves that echoes human sighs:
The time for living,
Both say, has been survived again.

46

In the darkness of this morning,
Between the barn and henhouse,
I stumbled over the carcass
Of my quickest cat.
It was as though my overboot
Had struck it dead.
The ceremony, following chores,
Was like the first bite
Into early rhubarb.
And even now,
Amid the lowering of evening,
I find it strange
That the sound of stealth
Could echo an emptiness
In so full a farm.

Yet here I sit,
Cold footed on a kitchen chair,
Counting the splotches on my hands.

Like a drunken mystic
I await their purr.

If after five more minutes
They have made no sound,
Or have grown no fur,
I'll have a glass of milk,
Then climb the shelterbelt
And with the sparrows
Try to relax.

47

Twilight:
A stray dog digging in the yard
not far from where a squirrel
stole a walnut.
A late hen collecting wayward worms.
A coyote singing of unsucked eggs.
And on the north porch,
near the woodpile,
Alvin Turner,
grinning like a gopher,
his loose flesh tilted on a chair:
recalling that
the closest thing
that Martha ever had
to hoarding
was her hair.

48

O the pleasure of rearranging bugs!
I sow the porches' undersides
With hedgeapples,
Trim the cabinets with sprigs of cedar.
Martha, waving lye-soap, shoos her kitchen clean.
And I remember one day
Playing detective,
Going squatheeled to shadow
The tortured line of insects:
They moved southward
Over clunkers huge to them
As mountains,
Over panicles and powdered leaves,
The softened needles of ages—
Over the clusterings
Of rock and shale,
Some pastern high,
Until,
Beside a walnut tree,
They dipped beneath the humping
Of a root,
And disappeared.

I had to smile when some years later
The mystery cleared.
It came with the noise
Of the walnut crashing,
With the warmth of the unshackled wood
That burned far cleaner
That winter than
Persimmon.

49

To yield
What you have never owned,
Then call it loss:
This is the turtle's puny voice,
The height of wilderness.

Why is it then
That the sweetest sound
I know
Is one unthrottled throat,
Crying?

50

When dampness trails me from barn to house,
Clinging like cotton underwear,
I shiver the skin like a hawsered stud
Impatient with horseflies.
But the chill is firmly fixed,
As deep as hair,
And in the night,
Half wrapped in featherbedding,
I entertain the vision of repose,
Stretching from floor to headboard
To pamper the moist aching.
The slipping toward sleep is as sweet,
As thick almost as syrup,
Warmed by the casual return
Of breath against the pillow.

There is much to be said for release,
For the putting aside of workboots:
Yet deep in the marrow a restlessness
Unleashes its gentle itch,
Defying even the dampness.
This Spring, it says,
Shall surely breed a bumper crop,
A granary closely calked.

At the edge of sleep
I see below a cow come fresh,
Licking her offspring clean.
While further down,
Beyond the scope of shiverings,
A single seed awaits its simple birth.

51

At the feedstore D. S. Simpson
Picks a roundworm from his teeth.
Or so it seems to me.
He has heard of cases just like mine,
Young man, he says:
The cow goes lean,
The circles at its eyes a toad-throat white.
And sometimes near the mouth
A swelling, soft as water.
They call it *bottle jaw*.
But with the proper schooling, he says,
And equipment,
You can spot the eggs,
Can see them in the victim's droppings.

Meanwhile the cow goes to her knees,
Then topples softly in the swampy lot.
And it is not the carcass
That I mind so much,
The leggy weight.
It is that I cannot hose
My bootsoles clean.

52

Observe the scene:
I, Alvin Turner, with his legions
Routing the stuck hog's punctured heart
In the direction of scalding.
The day, warm and vast,
And deeper than a horsetank,
Opens itself, it seems, to our necessities.

The hog by now does not object.

We hoist the steaming carcass,
Two legs spreadeagled
To a singletree
That creaks the branch it sways from.
The hog is emptied,
Scraped and quartered, salted and secured,
Until by bedtime only a rising wind
Is left to whine.
Relentlessly it hurries through the corn,
And rubbing lotion onto calloused hands
I suppose I overhear the stalk,
In its extremity,
Forgive the borer.

53

Shortly after the covering of Martha
I knelt at the edge of her grave,
Starched and heavy as a sashweight
Where the pallet should have been.
During the final weeks
I had taken to the floor beside her bed,
And now, at the turn of an aftermath,
I wanted some special word to leave her by.
The day had room for words, I thought,
Its topless sky like damp-ironed denim,
Workshirt blue.
From the cemetery hill
All treelines seemed remote,
And beneath my knee
The ground through thick green grass
Rose warm and firm, vast as a comforter.
Yet for all the room I left no word.
And I remember rising
To see what must have been
The reason why:
A crow half the height of a yearling,
Usurping the lawn.
I had grown its unsplit tongue,
And in the evening,
Back home at the hush of my acreage,
I began again by grunting single syllables.

54

Between them,
The bugs and the lightning
Conspired, in one season,
To harvest the walnuts.
Under a well-mauled wedge of light
The largest tree went halved.
Which seemed so very strange
The following morning,
In the sunshine, the stillness.
Like a freak,
Martha said,
And in spite of herself
Laughed.
And later,
At the moment of felling,
Like a neighbor who dropped from his tractor,
Heartstill and stiff,
The machine transected cleanly,
The relatives touching an empty seat
And with words recounting the growth rings.

55

At certain times
The time seems ripe for history.
I dredged that pond myself, I say,
And with horses.
To the boys, big eyed in bed,
I speak of scoop and scraper,
Of a daily spooning-out
Of rock and gumbo.
Like shot-sized sinkers laid on serried water
The mares, and me behind them,
Disappear.

Harnessed in words
The pond reshapes itself
Until at last I speak of rain.
But the boys are yawning now,
The time no longer right for history,
And to their balanced breathing,
And the fishing poles stood anxious in a corner,
I re-create the rain.
Again it runs downslope in rivulets
As long, as fat as sodworms,
Rutting the cowpaths
As they join themselves to join the cattle,
And a childish hope for catfish,
In the basin.

56

We are each one life
At the brink of one blocked quilt.

Earlier we said our vows.

Now we are alone,
Deluged with time,
The farm before us like another isle.

At the touching of hands
I know that much is well,
Though almost nothing matches.

Thus after lamplight,
In our mutual spell,
We bend ourselves to patchwork.

Both one, yet each a life.

I. Alvin Turner. Male. Farmer.
You. Martha. Female. Farmer's wife.

57

Had our firstborn lived
Would I have told her:
Observe the aphids,
Sweetheart,
On the clover?
I like to think I wouldn't.
I like to think my hands
As broad as curtains.
I open them to show the calf
Not scouring,
The corn not brown,
The pony with its rolling eye
Not coughing.
And that noise in the groin?
Why, it's only the windbreak working,
Honey,
Learning its music.

58

A length of wire
The size of Martha's clothesline
Hangs like a shepherd's crook inside the henhouse.
At the center of this familiar morning
I lift it from the wall,
A general pacing off his ceremony.

The first step, I tell myself,
Should be the least accountable.

Repeating this I snag the strutted leg
Of the most unmindful chicken.
My job is to bind the legs with twine,
To suspend the cockeyed victim upside-down.
Martha then will kill and scald
And pick the body clean,
Will cut/rinse/fry the pieces brown.
Surely this is as it should be:
Each to his own routine.
Dinner dripping from the clothesline,
The smoke of ready grease.

At the table I sit upright
Like a good soldier,
Home grown and responsive to orders.

59

Though Martha is small
I have yet to have to shake the sheet to find,
Or rouse, her.
Sometimes on an icy Saturday morning
Deliberately I calm her animation:
At such a time I view my hand as anvil,
And leaving it poised gently on her breasts
I slip away to do the chores.

And sometimes, sure enough,
I reappear to find the anvil holding,
With Martha's form beneath it, warm as cowflanks.
And O! these are the truly sweet, the sacred times.
The anvil gone,
The boys asleep,
The smell of milk and breath and chill
Against my woman.

60

To say *There is always the rock*
Is not to forfeit the harvest.
Below, beside each hard place
Lies the land,
Though I remember how one summer,
Wanting rain,
I watched my topsoil disappear in wind.
I called Martha to the south porch,
To the screendoor,
And told her the future, and my plan.
When the end arrives, I said
(And it is just around the corner),
Only rock will remain.
So I told her I'd fight it no longer:
To the conqueror goes everything.
Walking out and into the dust then
I released my hat,
Intending myself to follow it
To the remotest end of oblivion.
But my bootstrings,
Pesky with sandburrs,
Snagged the treetops,
So that when the ceiling cleared
I tumbled to rest in a plowseat,
And hitched to familiar mares.
After a recent shower then
The soil turned comic and dark.
On and within it the rock chuckled,
And no longer believing in wind
I joined their joke.
Now late into each year I work the ground,
Burying seedling and seed,
Stubble and husk and leaf.
That,
And the crushed dusty felt
Of the hat.